Internet Marketing For Teenagers (and younger)

Become an Online Superhero

Ian Richardson

ISBN-13: 978-1453864937
ISBN-10: 1453864938

Internet Marketing for Teenagers (and younger)

Become and Online Superhero

Published by:

Ian Richardson
http://AskIanRichardson.com

Thank you to Ellen Weston for her most excellent proof reading and editing skills.

ISBN-13: 978-1453864937
ISBN-10: 1453864938

Disclaimer

This book has been written to provide information to help you create your online brand and internet marketing business. Every effort has been made to make this book as complete and accurate as possible. Also, this book contains information regarding online marketing only up to the publishing date. Therefore, this book should be used as a guide – not as the ultimate source of online marketing information.

The purpose of this book is to educate. The author and publisher do not warrant that the information contained in this book is fully complete and shall not be responsible for any errors or omissions. The author and publisher shall have neither liability nor responsibility to any person or entity with respect to any loss or damage caused or alleged to be caused directly or indirectly by this book.

Message From The Author

Hello, I'm Ian Richardson and I've been using computers since before there was even Windows, even before there was Internet. Imagine for a moment using a computer that had a screen that was only one colour (green text) and after you switch it on all you see on the screen is:

C:>

That's it!

No instructions!

Nothing!

If you didn't know DOS (which stands for Disk Operating System) you couldn't get any further than that simple prompt on a screen.

Now many years later and a lot of education through my own studies, trials and errors I'm a lot more wiser (and older) about how to actually use computers and the Internet to make a living no matter where I live in the World.

My goal with this book is to help you with your quest to use the Internet and its unlimited possibilities to shape a future for yourself without the trappings of a 'regular job'. Don't get me wrong though, I'm not knocking regular jobs, I just know (like me) there are young aspiring entrepreneurs out there wanting to claim their piece of the Internet Pie which can turn the average 'geek' into a future millionaire if you just apply yourself.

I hope you enjoy what you will discover inside and let me know when you are appearing on TV as the next young millionaire.

IAN RICHARDSON

DEDICATION

I dedicate this book to my father who showed me that you get nothing without hard work, my mother who always said I had my head in the clouds, and to Cecilia who stuck by me through the tough times.

I also dedicate this book to all the young people who have a gut feeling they are destined for great things. NEVER GIVE UP the dream because one day it WILL be your reality.

Ian Richardson

Contents

1 - GETTING STARTED...1

2 - A SUPERHERO NAME 3

   Why You Need A Good Name 3

   You Will Be Noticed...4

   You Will Be Remembered 5

   People Will Talk About You..6

   Your Domain Name 7

   What Is Your Domain? 7

   Picking Your Domain Name..8

   Buying Your Domain..10

   Ways To Brand Yourself 12

3 – YOUR TRUSTY PARTNER 15

   The Basics of Webhosting 15

   Choosing The Best Web Host..17

   Price..17

   Traffic Control (AKA Bandwidth) 17

   Customer Service 18

   Reliability..19

   Security...19

Reputation 20

Flexibility 20

What About Web Design? 21

Finding Website Builders 21

What To Include On Your Website 23

Make A Website Right Now 24

How To Scare Customers Away 26

Other Help You Need 27

Website Designers 27

Writers For You 28

Your Own Contact Team 28

4 - MAKE A NAME FOR YOURSELF 29

How Search Engines Work 29

Drive People To You 30

What You Can't Do 32

Link Sharing With Others 33

Multiple Sites 34

5 – SPREADING THE WORD 35

Marketing 101 35

Why Market? 35

When to Market 36

Such A Thing As Too Much? 37

Mailing Lists..39

Why You Need Them 39

How To Build Them 40

What To Avoid...41

Autoresponders..42

What To Say 42

Autoresponder Strategies 43

Sales Letters 45

Why You Need Sales Letters 45

Where To Send Your Letter...46

Articles..47

What Do You Write About? 47

Where To Post Articles..49

The Local Media 50

Newspapers..50

Television Studios..52

AdWords..52

How To Sign Up 53

How To Maximize AdWords...53

Blogs 54

How To Create A Blog 54

What To Write.. 55

Information Products 57

Why People Want Information 57

Write A Book 58

Write A Report 59

Free Gifts? 60

Stickers 60

Magnets 60

Pencils And Pens 60

Forums 61

Where To Go 61

What To Say 62

6 - DOES A HERO GET PAID? 65

What Are Your Powers Worth?...................................... 65

Make Your Payment Schedule 66

Why You Need To Get Paid 67

Choosing A Payment System....................................... 67

What A Payment System Does...................................... 68

How To Choose Your Payment System 68

Security And Payments 70

Different Payment System Options.....................................70

A Donation System 71

Pay What You're Worth 71

How To Set This Up 72

Other Payment Options 73

7 - HAVE OTHERS TELL YOUR STORIES 75

Get Others To Help Market..75

Recruit Your Friends...75

Ask Around 76

Make It Worth Their While 77

What Are Affiliates? 77

Setting Up Affiliate Relationships.....................................78

8 - YOU CAN TELL YOUR STORY...79

Why Social Media Marketing Matters 79

Benefits Of Social Media 79

Tips And Tricks To Make Things Work 80

Social Media Options 81

Facebook 81

Twitter..83

9 - ALL IN A DAY'S WORK 85

10 – RESOURCE LIST 86

1 - GETTING STARTED

You want to do more with the Internet than just play games? You're not alone. While your parents might be using the Internet for their business, that doesn't mean you can't do the same.

In fact, there are many success stories involving children your age, figuring out how to maximize the tools the Internet already has to offer. Unless you have been living in a remote place with no contact to the world you will already know the story of Mark Zukerberg.... (Facebook). When I wrote this the value of Facebook was 25 Billion Dollars. Not bad for a young programmer hey?

Like an adventure game, you need to master certain skills in order to advance to the next level, where you can begin to really see the benefits of the Internet.

You can make money from being online and you can begin to see just how far the Internet reaches. While it might seem impossible to get the computer time you need, this doesn't mean that you shouldn't try.

After all, if your parents are always giving you allowance money, maybe it's time to do some work on your own so that you can boost your allowance and maybe even have the funds to loan your parents a few dollars every now and then.

(Not all the time, of course.)

You're going to begin the adventure of online marketing, something that has been done by many before you and many more that grow up along with you.

While there are a lot of steps to take, this doesn't mean you can't get started. Look at your Internet marketing plan as a way to recreate yourself as the hero in your lifetime – the superhero with money to spare.

2 - A SUPERHERO NAME

All of the great superheroes have had names that inspired others to fear them, or perhaps just to be intimidated by them. Regardless, you need to start thinking about ways in which you can create a name that not only makes other people think about you, but a name that makes them REMEMBER you.

Your superhero name doesn't have to be like the ones on the television or in the movies, though.

It can be even BETTER.

WHY YOU NEED A GOOD NAME

When you're reading an adventure story, you might notice that the main character in the book has a name that is easy to remember and, often, easy to pronounce.

Authors don't choose names randomly. They choose names because they will be memorable. Think about what would happen if all of those great stories about Batman were told about a guy named Phil. Not very memorable, is it? (No offence to anyone named Phil of course)

So you need to come up with a name for your Internet business that will allow you to be remembered.

There are a number of reasons why your Internet name should be memorable:

YOU WILL BE NOTICED

A good name is one that rolls off the tongue and gets you noticed when you walk into a room. Think about it: would you rather introduce yourself as Bruce Wayne or Batman?

A good domain name is what you will be using on your website – and probably for your business name too. So, since this name is going to be plastered all over the Internet, you need to make sure it's not only a little flashy, but also something that makes people take notice.

Some of the names that you already know from the world of the Internet include:

- **Apple:**
  While this name isn't highly flashy, it is a name that has been linked to cool products and new ideas.

- **Facebook:**
  What started out as a way to meet others 'face to face' in school has become a revolution, and it was actually first registered as The Facebook, later they dropped The to make it cleaner and also because most original users in University just kept referring to it as Facebook. So that is another thing to keep in mind as well.

- **Google:**
  This strange word is now used as a verb when a person talks about looking something up. *"Google it."*

- **YouTube**
  I'm sure you have visited YouTube and so do millions of other people every day. Not bad for something that started as an idea for somewhere to store videos.

You get the idea. The more noticeable your name is, the more likely your business will also get noticed, and that's how you're going to make money.

If you see a boring name, you probably wouldn't stop in the store, would you? Get noticed with a strong name choice.

All the reason above are why I picked Top Ranked Website for my business because it's not only the name of my business but it is also the service I provide and it's also good for keyword search. I use that as my "Shop Front", I also have a consulting business, Ask Ian Richardson.com and something I will keep after I have sold Top Ranked Website (which is part of my exit strategy), something you all must think about and have in place for any business.

YOU WILL BE REMEMBERED

Often, a good business is one that will be remembered over time. While it might be fun to be really popular for a short time, it's better to be popular over the long run.

You want to be popular not only today, but also tomorrow.

When you're thinking up a good name for your business and for your website, you need to start thinking about ways that you can stand out from the rest of the pack.

When you are remembered, you can:

- Always have new customers

- Keep loyal customers

- Spread the word more easily

- Maintain long term growth and money making

Being remembered sounds a little simple, but it's something that will allow you to earn money for a long time, and that's what you want.

When you are marketing on the Internet, there are many other people who are probably doing the same thing that you plan to do. When you are memorable, you will have people calling your name, just like they would for a superhero.

They will know who to call in an emergency...or just when they want to buy something.

PEOPLE WILL TALK ABOUT YOU

Now, most of the time you don't want people to talk about you, especially when they aren't saying good things, but when they are saying good things about you, you might want to hear what they have to say, and you want them to keep saying these things.

So, when you have a good domain name, you will begin to have people talk about you. They will start sharing stories about what you can do, who you are, etc.

While this doesn't sound like a big deal, the more people talk about you, the more they're going to want to find out more about you.

They're going to wonder who this Mr. X or Miss Y. person is and whether they are selling something they might want to buy.

The more people who talk about you, the more interest you will get. Even if only half of the people who talk about you are actually customers, this is still more than having no one talk about you at all.

In this case, you want people to talk about you – and that begins with choosing the best possible name.

YOUR DOMAIN NAME

Your domain name – sounds pretty cool already, doesn't it? – is something that will be linked to your business and to you for as long as you want it to be.

Though it sounds a little complicated, it's really not. This is something that is you already know plenty about. You just might not know how to get a domain name or how to make sure it's a good one.

WHAT IS YOUR DOMAIN?

Your domain is the name of your website online. For example, if you were Apple, then your website would be www.Apple.com. The text between the www and the other part is what your domain name is.

You can choose anything to be your website name, but you cannot use things like symbols in the website. So, you can't use www.$%.com. The domain name is basically the bookmark for your website.

This name allows you to have a place on the Internet and it helps you to be different from others who are also on the web.

For example, there is a big difference between www.apple.com and www.apples.com.

Just as the name you were given when you were born helps to set you apart from others in your life, you need to make sure that you are choosing a domain name that will set your business and your ideas apart.

You could also choose more than one domain name, if you like – and there are tricks you can use later on which will help you make the most of a number of names.

But one thing at a time.

PICKING YOUR DOMAIN NAME

You want to make sure that you are picking a domain name that:

- Is short.

- Is easy to remember.

- Does not include dashes.

- **That ends in .com**

These are pretty simple rules that will get you far when it comes to your domain.

First of all, domain names that are shorter will be easier for others to type and to remember. Think about how hard it would be to type out something like joeslemonadestand.com vs. joeslemonade.com.

You want to think about how easy you are making things for your customers.

Likewise, the easier the name is to remember, the better.

Dashes aren't necessarily easy for a person to remember when they are typing out a website name, so try to avoid these whenever possible, even if you think it will make your name easier to read.

It won't.

When you start looking at places to buy your domain name, you will notice that you have a bunch of different choices, including:

- .com

- .net

- .org

- .gov

- .edu

- .biz

- .info

Plus many others.

Though you might think some of the other ending parts sound better with your business name, you will want to choose .com whenever you can. This is a domain end that is respected and that will get you more attention than the others might.

(If you're not connected to a school or a government office, you shouldn't use .edu or .gov anyway.)

Now that you know you need to use a good domain name, it's time to pick one.

Here are some questions to ask yourself:

- What are people buying from me?

- Will my name be used for my business/website?

- Do I want to be catchy?

- Do I have a nickname I could use?

You will want to ask yourself these questions (and probably others) as you are picking out your domain name.

Something to keep in mind, you don't have to commit to just one domain name. In truth, it's really easy to buy additional domain names – and it's not that expensive.

All you need to do when you have another domain name is to create a link between the domains to ensure that when a person clicks on the link that they will get to the main site.

But, more on that later.

BUYING YOUR DOMAIN

If you're ready to buy a domain name, you need to head to sites that are reputable and helpful. Ideally, the domain name site should also be able to help you get an entire website setup. This is going to make things much easier for you and it's going to help you turn your ideas into reality.

You don't want to keep waiting to get your Internet adventure started.

Here is a list of places where you can buy domain names, but if you go to nearly any website building site, they will offer you the option to buy a website domain too. This is just making things so much easier for you and for anyone who wants to be online today.

- www.GoDaddy.com

- www.NameCheap.com

- www.CrazyDomains.com.au

Each of these sites will offer you the opportunity to buy a domain name before someone else does.

You will need some way to pay for the domain name, either a credit card or a PayPal account will work.

Here are some things to keep in mind when you're buying a domain:

- **Buy more than one:**
  You will want to buy as many domains as you can afford since this is going to give you more options. Try to buy at least two or three, if you have the money.

- **Look at the suggested domains:**
  When you go to purchase a domain, you will often get a list of related domain names. Look to see if there are any domains that might be a good fit too.

- **Buy short periods of time:**
  You can buy a domain for as little as one year. When you are first starting out, it's a good idea to reserve the domain name for no more than a year since you want to make sure you can be successful before you pay a lot of money. Though it is cheaper to buy domains for more than a year, this doesn't mean it's a better deal.

- **Consider private website measures:**
  If you don't want to have people finding out that you bought a website (or that your parent bought a website), you might want to look into creating a private domain registration. You will get this option during the buying process. It will cost more, but when you're younger than 18, you want to make sure people can't figure out where you live.

- **Don't buy anything else:**
  You are going to be shown a lot of things that sound like they're a good deal when you buy a domain. Ignore all other offers and

just stick to buying the domain name(s) right now. You have plenty of time to buy other things later on.

Buying a domain name shows you are serious about your Internet business and marketing.

This is a big step, so take a moment to pat yourself on the back.

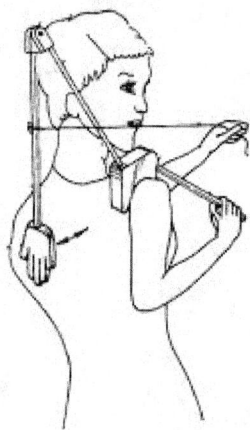

<u>WAYS TO BRAND YOURSELF</u>

Your domain name is the first way that you begin to create your identity in the Internet world. Just like a superhero, you need to create another identity that will cause you to get noticed.

Branding is something that businesses do all the time.

Think about Apple or about another large company. When you think about these companies, you might think of five words to describe them, and every time you think about these names, you associate those words with their products – no matter what they're selling.

You want to do the same thing. You need to create a 'brand' for yourself so that people automatically think of certain things when they think of you.

For example, if you are selling video games, you want to make sure your marketing will make you sound:

- Reliable

- Reasonably priced

- Fun

- Innovative

Now, these are just some basic words that everyone wants to use in terms of their brand. You might come up with other things

Right now, write down five words you want people to use when they describe your new company. These are going to be the foundation of your brand.

Now, once you have these words in mind, you can begin to create advertising and logos that help to remind the people who visit your site what you have to sell.

You can use branding in:

- The look of your website.

- Your slogan.

- The products you sell.

- The advertisements you create.

- The social media you use.

- The emails you send out.

- Anything that your customer might see.

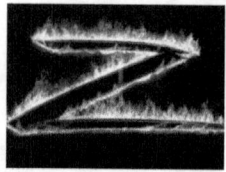 Think about it – whenever Zorro wanted someone to know that he was there, he would make the 'Z' carving, and in doing so, everyone knew that Zorro had been there.

While you're not going to carve letters into someone else, you can begin to create a brand for yourself by figuring out what you want others to say about you.

Over time, you might change this, but for right now, you need to make sure you know what your reputation should be. This is going to make it easier for you to create advertising campaigns and it's going to make it simpler for you to plan things from this point on.

Just like your domain name – how do you want to be known to your customers? That's your brand.

In this section, you've learned about domains, how to choose them, and the basics of branding your company. You're ready to take on some help to allow you to work even harder – without working harder at all.

3 – YOUR TRUSTY PARTNER

Just because you have a domain name doesn't mean you're ready to go. You need to start taking steps to ensure that you can be seen on the Internet.

You need a partner in crime, and that's where a webhost and good web design can step in.

THE BASICS OF WEBHOSTING

Webhosting is like having a partner to help you on your online adventure. When you buy a domain name, you will have a name that you can use, but this doesn't mean that you are going to be online.

Just buying that name means that you CAN be online. It doesn't mean that you are.

What you need is a webhost that will provide a space for you online. Think of this service as a way for you to have backup for when you're online. They are going to push other sites to the side so that you can be seen too.

When you get a good webhost, you will have a site that's always up and running and you will have a site that can handle any number of issues that come up.

There are several different types of webhosting from which you can choose, which does make things trickier.

- **Dedicated hosting:**
  This webhosting is the one that larger businesses use because

they don't want to share their web space with anyone else. This basically means that the website is on a particular server and it is not sharing the web space with anyone but itself. When the server goes down, the only site affected is the site that's on that server. Dedicated hosting is pricier, as a result, so it's something that you should think about carefully before signing up right now.

- **Shared hosting:**
  Or you might want to share the server with another website (or ten). This is an option when you don't have a lot of web traffic to worry about. At the same time, if one site on the shared server suddenly gets a lot of traffic to the site, that could cause the other sites on the server to not be accessible. This means that if site A suddenly gets bombarded with people, those who come to your site might not be able to see anything. Cheaper than dedicated hosting, you can see why it doesn't cost as much. Sharing is less expensive, but it can lead to troubles.

- **Free hosting:**
  Some people find that free hosting is the most tempting offer since it is, well, free. But sometimes you get what you pay for, and this is one of those times. Though free hosting might work for a while, it can also have a lot of problems, as the customer service might not be as good. In addition, the hosting might simply not be available one day, causing your website to disappear entirely from the Internet.

- **Reseller hosting:**
  If you really want to complicate things you could always become a host yourself. This way, you have the hosting space and you can sell it to others. Of course, this does mean you will need to have a good idea about what hosts do, how they work, and how to fix them when they go down.

Web hosting is one of the more complicated parts of going online and making a website. With so many choices and so many things to think about, it can take some time to make this decision.

It's important to choose a partner on which you can rely.

CHOOSING THE BEST WEB HOST

While there are many opinions about what makes up the BEST webhost, there are some things that you need to think about when you are making your own decision.

When you look at these options, then you can make the best choice for your needs and for your budget.

PRICE

When you're a younger Internet marketer, price does mean something. You don't have the large budget that other companies do and your mother or father might not want to spend the money that you need in order to give you a website up and running.

You will find that when you start looking at webhosts that the prices vary.

You can find plans that are as low as a few dollars a month or much more than this. Take some time to look at what each of these plans include before you settle on the right price.

This is an area where you don't want to be cheap.

TRAFFIC CONTROL (AKA BANDWIDTH)

Each time someone comes to a website, this causes a server to work harder than it did before the person came on the site. If the server isn't able to handle a lot of people, this means some people will not be able to see the site.

When this happens, it can make your business look bad. You want everyone who wants to come to your website to be able to find out and to buy from you.

As a result, it makes sense to sign up with a webhost that can handle more traffic than you think you will have. Try to purchase a webhost with medium traffic capability. This will allow you to manage the traffic flow and if things get crazy down the road, you can always upgrade your plan to something bigger.

But don't start out with the smallest amount of bandwidth. That's like only bringing one pizza to a party, even though you know that twenty of your friends will show up.

CUSTOMER SERVICE

Though you might not have to call customer service at all, you need to know that you can talk or email someone when there are problems. If you notice that your website isn't showing up online, you need to make sure that gets fixed.

If you can't talk to anyone, you will not be able to do anything to fix the problem – unless you're already a computer whiz.

A good way to find out if the webhost will help you with a customer service call is to call them up before you sign up with them. Talk to a person on the phone (or have a parent do this) to see how helpful they are and to see how they help you when there is a problem.

Though you might not have a problem at the moment, the customer service department should:

- Not put you on hold forever.

- Listen to your questions.

- Help you as best they can.

- Know what they're talking about.

If you get on the phone with the customer service department and they sound more clueless than you are, this is not a good sign.

You need to have this partner be available to help you with your problems.

RELIABILITY

You need to have a webhost that will be up and running as much of the time as possible. When a website is down, that means you are going to lose credibility with your customers. They're going to think you aren't a very good businessperson.

If a person comes to your site and sees a 'down' message more than once, it's likely they will never come back to your site.

You need to find a webhost that is available 99.9% of the time. Check with the company to see what their uptime rates are and then look online to see what the reviews of the webhost are saying too. Sometimes, the company might say one thing and real users will say something completely different.

You are counting on your webhost.

SECURITY

Though this might not be a big deal to you right now, you want to have a webhost that is secure. This means their servers aren't sitting out on a table in the middle of a room where anyone can tinker with them.

The servers need to be in a secure location, preferably underground or in a concrete building. This way, even if a hurricane hits, your website will still be up and running.

In addition, the webhost should have some sort of encryption to ensure that your website isn't going to be hacked by another person or company. You can check this security by asking the company what they use to keep websites safe.

If they don't use anything, keep looking for another webhost.

REPUTATION

Just like you might trust certain companies more than others, you need to see what the reputation of your new webhost is. All you need to do to check this is to:

- Search for reviews online.

- Look at other websites you like to see what hosts they use.

- Sign up for a trial period to see for yourself.

- Check with Consumer Reports and CNet to see what they say.

You need to check your facts before you start paying someone to broadcast your website online.

Though you might not be completely confident in your choice when it's time to make it, you will want to do as much research as possible to ensure that you've done all you can.

FLEXIBILITY

But what happens if you're not happy with your webhost? If you aren't happy with the reliability, you need to move your website to another host.

Is your current webhost going to make this difficult?

When you are looking into webhosts, ask them specifically what will happen if you decide to move to another host. Is this process going to be simple or is it going to cause you to have troubles switching?

You want to make sure that you can change your website, as needed. Though you probably won't have to switch if you pick the right host, this is something that might be on your list of questions to ask when you call the customer service department.

WHAT ABOUT WEB DESIGN?

With all of the focus on the webhost, what about your website? If you aren't making a cool website, why would anyone want to come to it anyway?

In this section, we're going to talk about the basics of how to build a website in just a few hours – a website that actually looks cool and will be something your customers want to visit.

FINDING WEBSITE BUILDERS

You can't be an Internet marketing superhero if you don't have a website, and while some superheroes are born with super abilities, you may not have been born with the ability to make a website.

The good news: there are tools that will do the work for you.

All you need to do is to find a few website builders online that will help you create a website in just a few minutes.

Some of the best website builders include:

- www.Hostgator.com:
  This is the hosting service I have been using ever since I got into serious business online. I have never had a problem and the

support is excellent. It has my HIGHEST recommendation. They provide a website builder, webhosting, and domain names.

- http://AsklanRichardson.com
  This is my own personal website building business where I can take you by the hand and help you build the exact site you need and if you mention having this book I will make sure to look after you.

- www.Weebly.com:
  This site is technically free, though you will have to buy a domain name to setup a website without the 'weebly' name at the end.

- www.VistaPrint.com:
  Here, you can buy a domain name as well as create a website, business cards, email marketing tools, etc. I didn't use VistaPrint for my website but I do use it for all other marketing material I use, and if you are smart like me you can save a HUGE amount of money on printing.

You want to choose website builders if you don't know how to create a website from scratch.

These sites will provide you with templates which you can then fill in with the things you like – text, products to sell, etc.

The main downside for these website builders is that you might not be able to change things too much. So, if you want the site to be black instead of the green on the template, you might not be able to do that.

If you want to make a website in a few minutes for not a lot of money, you can.

When you start to learn more about websites and how to build them, you can play with the HTML. (Don't worry if you don't know what that is.)

WHAT TO INCLUDE ON YOUR WEBSITE

But what do you need to include on your website? That's the trick. You need to think about what people want to read when they come to your website.

You want to make your site fun and engaging, but you also need to think about what's fun for the people who you imagine coming to visit.

Here are some ideas for your website, which you can then change to suit your own needs.

- **Home Page:**
  You need to have some sort of greeting on the front page of your website so that people can begin to know what you have to offer them or to sell to them. This should be a page that is inviting to read and that gives a basic overview of what the person can expect to find on your site.

- **About You:**
  Every person has a story, just like every superhero. Try to include your story on this page, making it as interesting as possible so that people can see why they should stay on your website.

- **What You're Selling:**
  Of course, if you're selling something, you need to list the items that you need to sell. This will help you make money and start to build a customer list.

- **FAQs:**
  If you find that people are asking you the same five questions again and again, you might want to put those questions and their answers on your site. This will save you time on emails that you get from customers.

- **Contact Information:**
  You will need to include some sort of contact information on your

website. This way, customers can ask you questions or let you know when they have problems.

Here are some fun extras you might also want to include:

- Traffic counter

- Message boards

- Forms

- Surveys and contests

- Photos

When you're first building a website, it's tempting to make things as complicated as possible. Don't do it.

You want to make your site no more than five pages or so when you're starting out. This will be easier for you to setup and to maintain.

Over time, as people begin to come to your site more, then you can begin to change things and make it more complicated.

MAKE A WEBSITE RIGHT NOW

You need to make your website as soon as possible. Once you choose a website builder, you can get started. Here are the basic steps to ensure you are making the best site possible in the shortest time possible.

 Personally I recommend using Wordpress for your website simply because it makes the whole process so much easier. Easier to build, easier to change, easier to manage. It is now the ONLY platform I use when building a site for clients and I have had NO problems at all.

- Choose your template.

- Choose five main pages to make. Add them to the design.

- Write out your web pages to cut and paste into the site template.

- Include pictures where appropriate.

- Add links into the text: This will vary from builder to builder, but in most cases, all you need to do is to highlight certain parts of the writing and then click a small chain link on the menu. Then you will be prompted to insert the link or link to another page on your site.

- Save your changes.

- View the site.

- Publish.

That's really all there is to it. Once you have the site up and running, all you need to do is to make sure that the information is still correct.

Over time, it's a good idea to change things around to ensure that you are creating something your visitors will find interesting. Since people come to a site again and again, you need to make things slightly different if you want to continue to engage them and to continue to help them with their needs. Think about one of your major supermarkets. Every now and then they will move stock around on the shelves. At first this may seem frustrating, but you continue to look for the product you want, and sometimes, you may see something new and decide to give it a try.

HOW TO SCARE CUSTOMERS AWAY

 Now, the problem for many online adventurers is that they get a little too excited when they see all of the things they can do on a website. They see that they can add a whole bunch of things to the design in order to make things fun.

But you need to stay away from a few things:

- **Too bright colours:**
  These will be hard on the eyes of some of the people who will come to your site.

- **Flash animation:**
  Not everyone can see the animations on their computers, so it's best to not include these on your site at all.

- **Too much information:**
  You don't want each of your pages to be three pages long. Try to keep your pages to no more than 500 words. People who are online want to read things quickly.

- **Too little information:**
  You need to explain yourself, what you do, and what you have to offer people.

- **Too many complicated words:**
  You will want to make sure you're writing as simply as possible, especially when you're selling something that might be difficult to explain.

- **Too few pictures:**
  People like pictures, not just words. Try to include images wherever possible. Not too many, of course.

You want to take some time to look at other websites that are selling similar items to the ones you are selling. This can give you ideas about what you should include – and what you should not include.

Remember, the best website is one that is easy to navigate and to use.

OTHER HELP YOU NEED

But an online adventurer might need even more help as they continue to market their ideas to the world.

That includes you.

WEBSITE DESIGNERS

While you might not need a website designer right now, there may come a time when you need to call in a professional to help you with your site.

Sometimes, you want to do things that are too complicated and that might cause troubles if you try to do them yourself. There are numerous website designers available through the website builder sites, as well as through freelance websites.

But this can cost anywhere from $250 and up, depending on how big and complicated you want your website to be.

This might be something you do when you are a bit busier.

You are always welcome to contact me to get your website built. Mention you have this book and I will make sure to give you the VIP treatment and price. www.AsklanRichardson.com

WRITERS FOR YOU

If you're afraid to write the pages for your website, you might want to hire professionals. One of the best services online and one I personally use myself is www.Articlez.com or you can find other freelancer websites at:

- www.Freelancer.com

- www.Elance.com

You will find people who you can pay to write strong website pages and entice people to come to your website – and to stay there.

YOUR OWN CONTACT TEAM

When you have a contact email or phone number (or both), you might need people to help you with responding to the calls and messages you get. Now's a good time to ask your friends if they want to be a part of your superhero journey.

You can pay them or you can treat them to a meal or some other surprise.

4 - MAKE A NAME FOR YOURSELF

What would happen if your website was the best in the world, but no one ever heard of it? What if you could fly in the air and no one knew that you could?

Nothing.

If you're not trying to make a name for yourself, all of the energy that you've spent making a website and coming up with a business idea will be wasted.

You need to learn how to get 'caught' in the World Wide Web.

HOW SEARCH ENGINES WORK

When you go online, you don't even think about how things work to help you find what you need.

Take, for example, when you're looking for a certain video game online. You type the name into the search engine and then you get a list of the stores that have the game available for sale.

It seems so simple to use.

So why are some sites on the first page of these search results while other sites are on the second or third page? When you are looking for games online, do you even read the other pages of the results after the first page?

Most people don't, and you probably don't either. It's just easier to read the first page. Those sites seem to be more reliable.

If you want your website to be on that first page, you need to realize how search engines basically work.

- The search engine matches the search terms to words found on websites.

- The number of those words on a website makes the match higher on the list.

But if it were really that easy, all you would have to do is to put as many of the right words on your website and you would get people to come to your site.

In fact, that's the way that things used to work. But now things are more complicated. Search engines have complicated math equations (that you don't need to know) that match up the search terms with the websites that are the best fit.

Nowadays, you can be smarter and you will make people notice you.

DRIVE PEOPLE TO YOU

You need to play by the rules in order to make sure that the search engine is your friend and not your archenemy.

- **Figure out keywords:**
  The first thing you need to do is to figure out what people will use in a search when they want to find something you are selling. For example, if you are selling cupcakes, you might make a list of keywords that include: cupcake, cupcakes, cup cakes, cup cake, desserts, etc.

- **Use keywords (a bit):**
  Once you have a list of the keywords that you think will be most popular, then you need to make sure these words show up on

most of the pages of your website. On each page, make sure these words are no more than 2% of the content. This sounds harder than it is. For every 500 words, don't use the one word keyword more than 10 times. All you need to do is to multiply .02 by the number of words on the page to get the number of times you can mention a keyword.

- **Use links:**
  You will want to include links in your website, as often as possible. These links should move a person to other pages on your website. For example, at the end of the home page, you can have a 'contact me' phrase that will be linked to your contact page. The more links you have, the more your website will be tangled in the World Wide Web.

- **Have good content:**
  You can't write web pages that don't make sense or that aren't helpful to those who read them. Make sure you are writing well, or pay someone else to do the work for you.

- **Update your website:**
  At least a few times a year, make sure you are updating your website and its writing. This will make it more exciting to those who visit it, as well as to the search engine.

- **Link to other sites:**
  You will also want to include a link list somewhere on your site. These links can be to friends' sites or they can be to other popular sites that are related to your website. This, again, will make your website seem more interconnected.

When you do all of these simple things, the search engine will rank you higher, and this will mean more people are going to find your website and see what you have to say.

With this increase in traffic, this will increase your search engine ranking even more.

Pretty cool, isn't it?

WHAT YOU CAN'T DO

You're probably trying to think of ways that you can begin to trick the system into putting you at the top of the search engine rankings.

You're not the only one.

But the truth is that search engines know when you are trying to be a villain instead of a hero, and if you try to press your luck, you might find yourself in a marketing snafu.

Here are the things you cannot do:

- Repeat the same keyword again and again for your content.

- Create pages that aren't seen on your site, but that contain nothing but keywords.

When you do these things and you're caught by your customers, they are going to think you're trying to trick them...because you are. This is going to ruin your reputation.

But if a search engine catches you doing these things, they can shut down your site completely. They will then blacklist you and you will have a hard time ever putting up a website again.

It's best to never learn how to do these things on your website. Wipe these ideas clean from your memory in order to be the 'good' website out there.

LINK SHARING WITH OTHERS

The more you can be connected online, the more you will be able to move up in the search engines.

Links are like referrals from people saying your website is good and you should visit. The more referral links you have the more the search engines will find your site and place it higher in their search results.

Here are some ways to do this:

- Look for other sites that complement your site,

- Ask their webmasters if they'd be willing to post your link if you post theirs.

- Post their link.

- Promote other businesses and their links.

- Have a list of links on your website that is updated regularly and checked to ensure the links are still working.

When you have links on your site, this will help to improve your rankings as well as to improve your reputation. When you're a website that promotes and helps other sites grow, you're going to get noticed.

At the same time, just because you put links on your website doesn't mean that the other site has to promote your site. So, don't take it personally if the other sites aren't as nice as you.

MULTIPLE SITES

You might also want to have multiple sites that have the same basic content, and these sites don't even have to cost a dime. All you need to do is to setup some free blogs that include the same content that you have on your main site and then link to each other by listing the links on each site.

This will boost your traffic and it can show you whether a blog works better than your site. If you have more people coming to your blog than to your 'normal' site, you might want to ask yourself why.

Here is a list of the various free blog services you can use:

- Blogger

- Wordpress

- Livejournal

- Blog.com

All you need to do is sign up for these blogging services and then you can begin to create posts.

These posts can be the same as your website or they can be related to your main website, helping you to cross-promote yourself and to drive traffic to your main site easily.

Just make sure you include the link to your main site.

5 – SPREADING THE WORD

Just when you thought you couldn't do any more to spread the word about your website powers, there's still more you can do.

You want to be the MOST FAMOUS website, don't you? That would be heroic.

MARKETING 101

Superheroes don't have commercials for themselves, so why should you have this sort of marketing too? Well, first of all, you don't need to have commercials in order to become more popular.

But you do need to have some marketing basics.

In order to make sure people know about you, they need to hear about you. That's where marketing comes in.

WHY MARKET?

You need to market yourself and your website for a number of reasons:

- More money

- More website traffic

- Long term success

It's pretty basic here. If you want people to come to your site and buy what you are trying to sell, you need to sell it to them. Having the best site in the world doesn't matter unless you tell others.

Imagine a superhero sitting at home, waiting by the phone. That doesn't happen.

It's been said that when you're trying to sell something most of your energy should be put into marketing and the rest will take care of itself, and it's the truth.

Imagine if a smaller company just stopped marketing. They wouldn't get new business, only the loyal customers would stick around. Even then, the old customers might think that the business wasn't doing well – and they might go to another business.

You have to market – no question about it.

Your business depends on it, and if you want to make money from business you have created, you need to make sure that you are marketing well.

WHEN TO MARKET

For many people who are first starting out, it can be confusing when you need to start marketing.

- Before people hear of you

- After people hear of you

The answer to this question is yes. You need to market at all times in your business' life. You need to market before the business takes off so that it does take off.

Once you're up and running, you need to make sure you're still marketing since you want new customers to always be knocking at your website's door.

The more you can expand your reach, the more you will be able to create a presence online. Just like the popular kids continue to be popular by doing popular kid type things, you need to keep marketing in order to make sure that you are staying in the minds of those you want to impress.

Here are some other times to ramp up your marketing:

- When you have a new product to launch.

- When you have a change in your website.

- When you're having a sale.

- When you're giving something away.

- When you have something new to offer – article, newsletter, etc.

Your marketing can be looked at as a super fast car that you might drive to get to the scene of a crime. It can go slowly, quickly, or super fast. But when it's parked, it isn't able to help you at all.

Think each day about what SPEED you want your marketing to be at. Then you can decide to do more or to do less, depending on what your current goals are for your website and for your business.

SUCH A THING AS TOO MUCH?

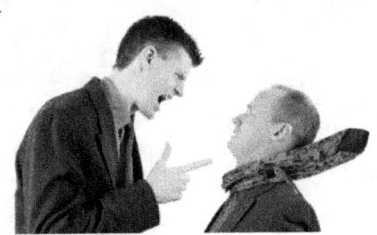

At the same time, you know how annoying commercials can be. You don't want to be too market-y and begin to scare new and old customers away. You need to get the marketing just right.

But how can you tell when you're doing too much?

- Your sales drop off.

- People begin to complain.

- You are marketing something new every day.

- You are constantly switching your marketing strategies.

You don't want to market more than once a week in your business since you probably don't have a lot of new things to offer regularly. In time, you might need to tell your customers new things more often, but at this point, you might want to hang back and let the customers see what you have NOW.

In time, you will present new things to them.

This is when you can begin to use these other marketing techniques.

If you do too much at once, you're going to get confused about what is working and what isn't. That's going to cause you to guess the next time you have to do some marketing.

Instead, try a few things, see how they work, then try more.

MAILING LISTS

You know about junk mail – we all do. But this isn't what we mean when we talk about mailing lists.

Mailing lists are an essential tool for online adventurers. When you want to reach out to as many people as possible, you need to reach as many people as possible.

A mailing list can be:

- A list of email addresses

- A list of snail mail addresses

These lists are basically opportunities and chances. Like buying a lottery ticket that may or may not pay off, these addresses can help you to get more traffic to your website and to get more people to pay for what you're selling.

But you need to know how to get them and how to use them. They are an essential tool on your adventurer tool belt.

WHY YOU NEED THEM

But what do mailing lists allow you to do? When you've gotten someone's email address, for example, you can:

- Send them a thank you note for an order.

- Reply to their questions.

- Send them a coupon for their next order.

- Send them a newsletter.

- Send a special announcement about a new change or product.

- Send them insider deals.

- Send them a link to an article, blog, etc.

Mailing lists help you extend your reach beyond your website. While your site can reach a lot of people, when someone signs up for your mailing list, they are more than just interested in your site.

They want to buy from you. Why else would they want to listen to more from you?

Mailing lists give you the chance, again and again, to try to sway a reader into doing what you want them to do, which is to hopefully get them to buy what you're offering to them.

HOW TO BUILD THEM

You can create mailing lists more easily than you think. When you're creating your website, look for the option to add on a form. You can turn this form into a place where a person can sign up with their email address.

In exchange for their email address, you might want to say:

- We will mail you on occasion with special updates and coupons, or...

- We will mail you with our semi-weekly newsletter, or...

- We will mail you with the latest happenings on our site.

You get the idea. Try to make it enticing for someone to give you their email address. You need to let them know they are going to get something good in return for their email address.

You know that you've given your email address to some companies, only to get a bunch of junk in your email box.

You need to be someone who sends their mailing list something special and something the reader can actually use.

Other tips for building your mailing list:

- **Give away something:**
  If you offer a freebie to people for giving up their email address, then you might get more addresses.

- **Offer special access:**
  You might want to allow people who give you their email address access to other sites that you have hidden away.

- **Create contests:**
  People love to win things. By offering a prize during a particular time, you can gain a large list of email addresses in the process.

Or you can just ask your friends to give you their email addresses and then they can tell others to do the same.

That works too.

WHAT TO AVOID

When you have a mailing list at your fingertips, you don't want to abuse this power. It might be tempting to send your mailing list new messages every day, but this is just going to make people upset they ever gave you their address in the first place.

Here are some other things you need to avoid:

- Sending spammy messages.

- Sending information that is boring.

- Sending specials and deals every day.

- Sending messages with bad links in them.

- Sending messages that are always trying to sell.

You want to create a relationship with the people who are getting your mails, not just try to sell things to them.

Think about the things you hate when you sign up for mailing lists on sites – and don't do those things.

It's very important you always take people off the mailing lists when they ask – immediately, if possible.

AUTORESPONDERS

When you have a mailing list, you can also set up autoresponders. These are emails that come at regular intervals in order to slowly talk a person into buying from you – or at least to get to know your website better.

These series of emails are not chain letters, but they should be useful to the person who is reading it.

If not, they're going to get sent to the spam folder, along with your business' reputation.

WHAT TO SAY

When you're not sure what to put in your autoresponders, here are some things you can do to make things interesting and worthwhile:

- **Create seven-day courses:**
  Each day, the person will receive a new lesson about something that is related to what you are selling.

- **Create a yearlong mailing:**
  Each week, the person can receive a new tip for using their product or for doing something related to your website.

- **Create a story that continues at regular intervals:**
  Even if your website is just to show off a story or a movie idea you have, you could use autoresponders to begin to send bits of the story to those who have signed up.

- **Create a book long program:**
  If you have something more detailed to tell people, then you can create an autoresponder series that will give lots of detailed information and links to help them learn.

As you can see, the programs are all meant to build on the week or the month before. In doing so, you will keep the interest of the reader and this will encourage them to continue to stay on the list to find out more.

When they continue to read the mailers, they will eventually be more likely to buy something from you.

Autoresponders build trust and they build a connection between you and your customers.

AUTORESPONDER STRATEGIES

When you are mailing out autoresponders, you need to make sure you are following a few simple strategies that will help you to be more effective.

- **Only send good information:**
  You can't send so-so information and expect people to enjoy reading your emails each time. You need to send solid information each and every time. Each mailing needs to offer something that will help the other person.

- **Make sure the emails are error free:**
  While you might believe you are a good writer or editor, it's never

a bad idea to have someone else look at your work. This will ensure that your mailings don't send the wrong impression. They can be forwarded to others, after all.

- **Encourage forwarding:**
When a person receives your mailing and they think it has worthwhile information, encourage them to send it to someone else. This will increase your mailing list and your customer base.

- **Include your website link:**
Every mail should have your website link in it. This will ensure that you are able to create traffic that comes to your website more often.

- **Give the person a chance to stop the mailings:**
The end of every mail should have a chance for the person to stop receiving the mailings. Sometimes, people will just want to slow down the flow of information to their in box.

- **Sign up for autoresponder services:**
If this all sounds too complicated, you can always pay someone else to do this work for you. You can hire a writer to write the series and you can pay for a service to send out the emails to your mailing list (www.Aweber.com, for example, is just one of the companies which can do this).

Autoresponders are marketing disguised as good information. Not only are you connecting with customers, but the more worthwhile the information, the more likely you are to encourage the reader to buy something too.

SALES LETTERS

Many Internet marketers think that sales letters are the key to their success. You can use these too, like another weapon in your adventurer arsenal.

Sales letters are marketing at its best and at its most effective. They talk directly to the customer about what they want, and by connecting in this way, those who read the sales letters are more likely to make a purchase.

WHY YOU NEED SALES LETTERS

There are a number of reasons why every Internet marketer should use sales letters at some point of their marketing campaign.

- **They're easy to write:**
  You can go online right now and find a sales letter. Read it and then try to write your own based on how the other person did it. Don't copy it, of course, but you will see how easy it is to write one of these pieces.

- **They're popular:**
  Most of the bigger online companies will use a sales letter of some sort. So when you use one, it's not going to seem out of place or too pushy.

- **They give information:**
  A well-written sales letter is one that gives the reader a lot of information about the product or about the idea that is being promoted. This isn't just a fluffy piece.

- **They are great landing pages:**
  Sometimes when you click on a link to a certain product, you might find yourself on a sales letter. This letter includes a lot of details about what the product does before you are directed to the actual site. You have 'landed' on the sales letter page, but you will not stay there if the sales letter does its job.

- **They are low pressure:**
  When you read a sales letter, it's more like it's talking to you and to your needs than selling anything to you. It's going to be most effective when it discusses what you need and then talks about how the item being sold can provide those things. Only at the end of the letter is a person directed to do something in order to take action.

Sales letters are something you can use now and for any future plans you have for your website.

WHERE TO SEND YOUR LETTER

Your sales letter doesn't have to be something that you use as a landing page either. This can also be something that you send to people on your mailing list.

Ideally, you want to only send this sort of page to your mailing list if the product being sold is new and the mailing list would not have already heard of it.

Otherwise, it might seem a little boring and redundant.

You can also use this sales letter as its own website. This is where those extra domain names can come in handy. When you have more than one address, you can put your sales page on that domain and then link to your main site at the end where it says 'If you want to learn more, go here.'

This will direct traffic to your site, while also helping to create a smoother transition from information to action.

You might also be able to send a toned down version of this letter to a newspaper or an online blog, but this might be a little too sales-y for some, so this isn't the first thing you want to do.

ARTICLES

What many people don't realize is that knowledge is power, and even though you might hate school right now, it's something that is going to help you for the rest of your life.

Your website needs to be able to inspire confidence in those who read it.

Think about it. If a superhero doesn't seem to be that smart, do you think you'd call that superhero when you were in trouble? Probably not. You'd probably run the other way from trouble since the person is probably someone who can't help you.

When you write articles and you share them with your customers, you will show that you are smart and that you are someone who can be trusted to tell them what they need to know.

Internet adventurers use them every day.

WHAT DO YOU WRITE ABOUT?

But the main question that most people have is what you would write about when you create articles.

The answer? Anything.

You want to write about things which are related to your field and to the website that you are promoting.

For example, if you are selling video games on your website, you might want to talk about how to beat the latest version of a game or you might want to review the latest game to share your opinions.

Your articles are YOUR articles, so they can be about anything.

Here's what you should include in order to be the most effective for your customers and audience:

- Instructions to do something.

- Advice about a certain topic.

- History about a topic.

- Quick tips and strategies.

- Reviews of products.

You want to write an article that actually teaches the reader something new or maybe just something they can use.

Here are some ideas for topics:

- How to do something on a budget.

- How to plan something.

- How to create something from scratch.

- How to find something.

As you can see, these topics can be adjusted to nearly every topic and idea that you might have, and this is a good thing.

You should have a number of different things you can write. In fact, you might want to create a list that you can keep near you, adding to it as you begin to get ideas.

At the end of all of your articles, you need to include:

- Your name.

- Your website link.

- A quick bio: For example, "Joe Smith is from Chicago and enjoys putting together model ships when he's not parasailing."

This link at the bottom will serve to drive traffic to your site, helping you not only with your website reputation, but also with your ability to have more customers come to your site to learn more.

WHERE TO POST ARTICLES

You can post articles in a variety of places and often for free. You just need to look into the different publishing guidelines that the sites offer so that you can make sure you're following the rules.

- www.EzineArticles.com

- www.buzzle.com

- www.hubpages.com

- www.examiner.com

- www.akgmag.com

- www.eHow.com

But this is not a comprehensive list. You can go online and find other places where you can post your articles for free.

Once you have written some articles, you can post them at all of these sites in order to spread out your website link and your information.

Remember, your articles need to be:

- Factual, not sales-y

- Free of spelling errors.

- Free of grammar errors.

- Free of factual errors.

- Easy to read.

You want to make sure you're not posting anything longer than a page since people who are online would rather spend less time reading, than more time reading.

Also, if your articles are a success, you can turn them into an online course, an autoresponder series, etc.

The possibilities are endless.

THE LOCAL MEDIA

Of course, when you really want to get people to notice you, you might want to turn to your local media to help you out.

While it might seem like only the big companies get on TV, since you're younger, your story might be better than most other stories. You might find it really easy to get your story on the air, even if you don't think you have a lot to say.

Years ago when I started my first business I was in my early 20's and really didn't think what I was doing was something the local newspaper would be interested in. After being encouraged by a business I did some work for I contacted the local newspaper and to my surprise I got a large article and photo in the paper. This of course lead to a number of calls and new clients.

NEWSPAPERS

The newspapers in your area would love to cover a younger person like yourself in their paper, and it's going to be much easier to be a part of the paper and get yourself known.

What you want to do is to contact the newspaper over email or on the phone to ask how you can get your business covered in the paper. Make sure you write out what you're going to say and what you want them to say about you before you begin to talk on the phone or in the email.

You could create a list of answers to these questions:

- Who you are

- Where you're located

- What you do

- Why you're doing what you're doing

- How you're doing what you're doing

- When you began your business

This way, you will have the answers the reporter will ask.

If you can't seem to get through to a reporter, you could also take some time to write up a press release. Don't worry, this is easier than it sounds.

Here are some tips to write up a press release:

- **Include the date it needs to be released:**
  Hint, since this probably isn't horribly important or time sensitive, just use the current date.

- **Include a strong title:**
  You want to write something that will get the attention of the person reading it.

- **Do not write a sales piece:**
  A press release should just give the facts about your website and/or business, who you are, what you do, etc.

If you do end up getting a hold of someone at the newspaper, they might have you write up your information in another way, so make sure you follow the rules you hear, not just the rules in this book.

TELEVISION STUDIOS

You may also want to call up the local TV station to see if they might want to do a story on you and on your business. You never know whether they have airtime they might need to fill.

Most likely, they may call you back to fill in a Saturday or a Sunday spot. Make sure that you are flexible as to when your story might be covered.

Just call the local news station, tell them what you have to offer or you can email the station manager with the press release you've just created for the newspapers.

ADWORDS

To further spread the word about your online business and you want to market by spending money instead of using free resources, there is plenty more you can do.

Google AdWords is a system many businesses use in order to advertise around the web without having to do anything more than create a few advertisements.

HOW TO SIGN UP

To sign up for AdWords, all you need to do is to create an AdWords account. You can do this when you sign up for a Gmail account by going to this site:

http://adwords.google.com

If you already have a Gmail account, this is going to be quick and easy. You just need to follow the instructions to create your AdWords account, and then you will go through an eighteen-step process to start your advertising campaign.

The basic gist of AdWords is that you will create ads using keywords that Google will select.

The more popular the keyword, the more often it is searched, so this marketing tool will charge you more to use ads with that keyword.

You can create ads with any keywords that fit your website and then you will set a certain amount of money to use for your campaign each day. When this money is out, your ads stop running.

This allows you to set a certain amount of money for advertising, but this also means that you will have to have money to spend.

For most people, you don't have to use AdWords until you are already making money. Then it's worth it.

HOW TO MAXIMIZE ADWORDS

When you are signing up for AdWords, you will often get a $100 gift certificate in the mail to try out a campaign in order to see how it works for you. Use this coupon.

Set up a campaign or two, based on the most popular keywords you can buy. Following Google's instructions, build your campaign to fit your needs and then see what happens as a result.

You can follow along with the success of your campaign by going to the Google Analytics page in the AdWords menu. This is just a chart that tells you how the ad is doing, if people are clicking on it, and whether it's a success or not.

This allows you to quickly see if the money you're spending is worth it.

BLOGS

You already learned about how blogs can be helpful for online adventurers. But you haven't really learned how to create an effective blog, one that will help to sell your business and the ideas you have.

These free tools are being used by many, and they can be used by you too.

HOW TO CREATE A BLOG

All you need to do is to use one of the many free blogging platforms that are available. These tools will guide you step by step to make a blog, even one that can show off your personality.

Here are some tips to keep in mind as you are building your blog.

- Use the same name for the blog as you do for your websites.

- Use the same sort of colours as your webpage uses.

- Make the blog simple.

- Include a link to your main web page.

- Include a picture of yourself or your business logo.

While this seems like a quick set of instructions, this isn't something that you want to spend a lot of time on.

A blog should be something that should be set up in just a few minutes. You will create the blog and then all you need to do is to add in blog entries.

A few rules when creating a blog and using a blog include:

- **Write often:**
  There's nothing more frustrating than going to a blog for a while and enjoying the content, only to watch the time between posts get longer and longer. If you want to use a blog, you need to make sure you're writing for it as often as possible.

- **Use your voice:**
  You want a blog to be a little more casual than your regular website. This is a place where you can show off your personality. Think of this as your TV room while the website is the dining room of the house.

- **Use pictures:**
  You can add pictures with most blogging platforms, so make sure you do this. You want to make the blog fun to look at, not just a lot of things for people to read.

WHAT TO WRITE

But the real question is what to write about when you have a blog. After writing articles, a website, autoresponders, and more, you might be out of things to say.

Well, you could always post the things you post on one site on all of your sites.

Of course, some people will catch onto this, so you might want to add something that's a bit more unique.

Here are some ideas about what you can include in a blog that will be worthwhile for people to read, while also being interesting enough to keep someone coming back:

- **Multi-part series on how to do what you do:**
  If you are trying to teach someone something through your business and your website, it might be a good idea to create a whole series of blogs that will help to teach someone something step by step.

- **Different daily blogs:**
  For example, you might have Mondays be about a certain topic every single week. This way, people know to come to your blog on Mondays when they want to learn more about that particular topic.

- **Different parts of your life and business:**
  If you want, you might want to introduce pictures from your house and other pieces on what makes your business run.

- **Opinion pieces:**
  If you find a book that you enjoyed that relates to your website, you may want to review it on your blog or talk about other things you've learned that you have an opinion on.

A blog is a much more open space in which people can be certain to learn more about you as well as more about things that are going to help show that you are someone to listen to.

Just write one.

INFORMATION PRODUCTS

If you notice with many businesses online, they not only sell the things they want to sell, but they also offer things like eBooks and reports to their customers.

These added products can not only bring in money, but they also help to show that you are an expert in what you are talking about, and the more you can show you are an expert, the more others will listen.

WHY PEOPLE WANT INFORMATION

People always want to learn more, even if they understand the basics. There will always be more questions, more concerns when it comes to anything, so the more information you can offer, the better.

People want information because it may:

- Help them do things better.

- Encourage them to look at things a new way.

- Let them know they are not alone.

- Tell them something they don't know.

- Cause them to do their own research about something.

People like to have information as well because it helps them feel as though they're making the best decision when they buy something.

When you buy a computer, for example, you don't just buy the first one you see (hopefully). You take time to learn all that you can before you make a purchase like that.

To be a hero to someone, you need to provide them with the same sort of information.

You need to be able to provide them with all of the necessary information so they are confident that they are making a purchase that is right for them and that will help them out.

WRITE A BOOK

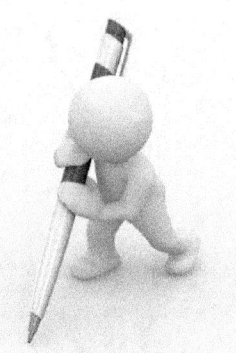

One of the most common ways to provide information is through an eBook. This is a book that is transmitted digitally and that does not come in a printed form.

The book offers sound advice and information on any given topic, in the hopes that reading the book will encourage the person to make a purchase or to begin to look at a website in the future.

Some people like to charge for the eBooks they write, while others just give them away in order to encourage people to buy something. Or the eBooks might be given with an order, encouraging people to buy something in order to get the eBook.

You can write an eBook about anything related to your website or the things you want to sell to someone else. This might be an instructional book, a history book, a factual book, etc.

The book simply needs to include something that will help the person who is reading it learn more.

Some great things to include in an eBook include:

- Links to outside resources the reader can use.

- Lists and bullet points for easy reading.

- Images and graphs where appropriate.

- A clear table of contents for easy reading.

You can also include a short biography of yourself as well as another link to your website – it never hurts to put this in as many places as possible.

WRITE A REPORT

If the thought of writing a book is a little overwhelming, you can also look into writing a report.

This can be just a page or so of information that you hand out to people on your website for signing up for your mailing list or for making a purchase of any kind.

Some ideas for a report include:

- Top Ten Ways to _____.

- The Five Reasons You Should Always _____.

- Quick Ways to Clean Up Your _____.

- The Four Most Common Problems of _____ (And How To Fix Them).

These reports can be pieces a person can read in as little as five minutes, but they can get a lot out of them.

You can create different reports for different topics or you can simply change the reports from time to time with updated information if things should change.

FREE GIFTS?

Everyone likes free stuff, don't they? The more stuff you can hand out for free, the more likely people are going to turn to you to be their personal online adventurer.

You might be able to mail these things to people when they sign up for your mailing list or you can give them out to friends who can just pass them onto everyone.

STICKERS

Stickers with your website name and business name are always fun to hand out – and they're cheap to make on any computer. Just make sure they are fun to look at or a person might not want to stick it anywhere but in a drawer.

MAGNETS

Magnets are something that people can use on their fridge at home, so these are helpful as well as effective for spreading the word about your business.

PENCILS AND PENS

You can order pencils and pens with your company name and website address on it. These are also useful, cheap to buy, and cheap to send to customers.

While you don't want to give everything away for free, sometimes when you're first starting out, it's the best way to begin to show others that you have something they want to buy.

A great place to get all these promotional items printed with your information is www.VistaPrint.com.

FORUMS

Superheroes today can certainly use the Internet to promote themselves —and one of the places they should do are the forums.

There are forums all over the Internet, helping people connect in order to talk to each other and to learn more about what the other person knows and wants to share.

Forums are a good place to take your marketing since:

- Forums are free.

- Forums are where your customers are.

- Forums are everywhere.

- Forums allow you a place to show your expertise.

On these sites, discussions have already started and you can either start your own or join in with the others who are talking about what you want to talk about too.

WHERE TO GO

If you type into any search engine a keyword from your website and 'forum,' you are bound to run across one or more forums about your topic.

Here, you will want to register and look around to see what others are talking about.

Usually, there will be a long list of the discussion topics that are being discussed at the time as well as the number of people who have responded or viewed the discussion.

You can sign up for one or for many of these forums, though being involved in more forums is always the better choice. You want to make sure that you are creating as many opportunities for yourself to be a part of the 'in' crowd.

Online adventurers need to speak up in order to be heard.

WHAT TO SAY

When you are on these forums, it is tempting to just talk about yourself and about the things you have to sell to others.

Avoid doing this.

Here are some tips to make sure you are being a good forum member and not someone who will be ignored or banned.

- **Listen to what others are saying:**
  When you're on the forums, take some time to listen to what others have to say to you and around you. You want to see what's important to others who are talking, not just be the one who talks all the time.

- **Answer questions you can answer:**
  If you see someone has a question, try to answer it if you are able to answer it. This will help the other person see that you are a helpful person.

- **Ask questions when you have questions:**
  If you have a question, be sure to ask the question. You will look like you're another forum person, not just a business that wants to find more customers.

- **Include your website link, if possible:**
  At the end of each post, it's usually possible to put your website link in your signature. Just check the rules to make sure this is the case.

- **Be willing to be wrong:**
  If you say something in the forum and someone corrects you, admit when you are wrong. This will encourage others to see you as every other person. You will not seem defensive or angry.

- **Be active in the forum:**
  You want to post as often as possible to show that you are interested in the topic and willing to be a part of the conversation, even when you're not talking about your business.

Forums are a great place for ideas too. The more you listen, the more you can learn about what to do for and with your business.

6 - DOES A HERO GET PAID?

In the movies and on TV, you don't see superheroes get paid for the work they do.

Being a hero is a thankless job and one that seems to be harder than the one that you're doing right now. But you can still get paid for the work you do.

If you are selling a product or you are selling a service, you deserve to be paid for this. This time, the online adventurer does get to take home some money after a hard day's work.

WHAT ARE YOUR POWERS WORTH?

Your powers are something that you should charge for. After all, websites don't build themselves. But many people who are starting out in any business have troubles deciding what to charge, what is enough, what is too much, etc.

This section is going to cover the basics of making sure that you're charging enough and that you're getting paid well.

MAKE YOUR PAYMENT SCHEDULE

A payment schedule is something that will show you exactly what to charge for things that you sell.

For example, if you sell boxes of crayons, the chart will show you what a pack of 12, 24, and 48 will all cost to your customer. Also on this chart should be the actual cost of product when you bought it.

If you paid $1 for a 48 pack of crayons, you need to charge more than $1 if you want to make some money.

One of the most common ways that people choose the prices for their products is to 'keystone' their prices. What is this? This means that for every dollar that you spent buying something, you will charge $2.

You are marking up your prices 100%.

This means that you will always make a profit on the item, even if you decide to have a sale.

If you decide to have a 25% off sale, this is what would happen. An item you paid $5 for would be regularly priced as $10. During the sale, you would charge only $7.50, which means that while the prices are lower, you're still making money.

You don't have to follow this sort of pricing chart, but you might want to come up with something that is easy to remember, and charging double what you paid is pretty easy to remember.

You can get out a piece of paper and write down all of the prices that you can expect to charge your customers and then it's as simple as transferring those prices onto your website.

WHY YOU NEED TO GET PAID

You might be nervous about asking for money, especially since you're younger, but you are running a website and you are marketing something to someone else. This means that you will have things you need to pay for, and that takes money.

You need to get paid in order to pay for:

- Your website costs.

- Your web host costs.

- The stock you have to buy.

- Your office supplies.

- Your shipping costs.

- Etc.

You get the idea. It costs money to make money. Superheroes even have normal jobs – Clark Kent, for example. It takes money to live in the world, and you need to get paid.

CHOOSING A PAYMENT SYSTEM

So, how can you begin to take money from people who are willing to buy what you have to sell?

This is the part that trips up adults just as much as it might confuse you too. When it comes to a payment system, you need to create something that will be able to take money from others in a safe way.

It doesn't have to be hard at all. But the more you can make it simple, the more easily you will collect money and be able to create a business that can work even when you step away from the computer.

WHAT A PAYMENT SYSTEM DOES

A payment system will take the money from the person that is buying things from you during a few simple steps:

- It takes the order.

- It totals the order.

- It charges tax, as needed.

- It calculates shipping costs.

- It collects the money.

- It sends the money to your bank account.

This system works within second, helping to be another trusty sidekick who will be there to ensure that your online adventures can continue.

But even more important is the idea of providing you with a secure way to take money. You don't want to take a payment from someone, only to learn later that your customers had their financial information stolen.

HOW TO CHOOSE YOUR PAYMENT SYSTEM

A payment system can be really complicated or it can be simple. Since you can't actually setup a payment system without an adult, you will need to talk with a parent about what they're comfortable with.

Together, you can look at some payment systems and then begin to choose the one that seems to be best for your online business.

Here are some of the things to keep in mind as you choose your payment system:

- **Pricing:**
  Funnily enough, payment systems do cost money to use. You need to make sure that you are clear about how much you will be using the payment system in order to see how much it might cost. The fewer items you sell, the more expensive the system might be, though if you have a system that is per charge, then you might be able to spend less. Take some time to compare the different prices that are available and the plans that you could use.

- **Flexibility:**
  You want a system that is going to be able to take more than one type of payment. If you can only take one kind of credit card, but a customer has another credit card, you won't make any money. At the least, you should be able to take Visa and MasterCard.

- **Compatibility:**
  The payment system should be able to be installed on your website without any troubles or issues. A simple link or an HTML code should be easy to use and easy to include in the coding (or as the help desk of your website design site what you need to do).

- **Control:**
  You want to be able to see how your payment system is working, so if you're not able to access the system on your own, this isn't going to be a good fit. Make sure you can look at the program behind the scenes.

- **Security:**
  Security is really important, even if you feel you have done everything else right. The system should have many layers of encryption and SSL technology to make sure all payment information will stay private.

Looking at more than one payment system is ideal. You and your parent should actually look at four systems, at the very least. This way, you can make sure you have investigated all of your options.

SECURITY AND PAYMENTS

Security is something you can promise to your customers, but can you deliver it? Can you imagine what might have happened to Superman if he promised he could save Lois Lane and then didn't?

People wouldn't come to him anymore.

When you want to make sure your customers feel safe enough to buy from you, you need to ensure that your payment system is secure.

Ask the company what they do to make sure the payment information is safe when it moves from a customer to the payment system. Is the information encrypted? When it is decrypted? What happens to the information once it's been used?

You will also want to check to see if there have been any major breeches in the security of the payment processor system so that you can see how they handled the situation and how they will prevent it in the future.

Those companies that messed up might seem to be companies to avoid, but it's not often that companies make the same mistakes twice.

DIFFERENT PAYMENT SYSTEM OPTIONS

There are a number of different ways you can take payments and process them in order to fill up your online adventurer bank account.

Some of the most popular include:

- PayPal.com

- ClickBank.com

- 2CheckOut.com

Take your time and look at the hundreds of possibilities that are out there. You might be surprised at what you find that will work for your specific needs.

A DONATION SYSTEM

Another possible way to make money from online marketing and your website is to think about a donation system. While this sounds like a crazy idea, it can actually work well since it allows people to pay what they think you are worth.

PAY WHAT YOU'RE WORTH

This system is like the honour system in school. You get something from someone else, but you promise to pay him or her back. If you don't pay them back, then you are considered to be stealing. Since everyone has agreed to pay, then most people will.

In the donation system, what you will do is create a time of year (or a few times a year) when you will ask people who read your blog or your site to donate money to you.

What you can do is send them a newsletter each week when they sign up for your mailing list. After a year's worth of newsletters, then you can ask for a donation based on what they think the information was worth.

Not only will you get paid by them, but you will also find out if your newsletter is any good.

While you might feel strange about asking for money, you might be surprised at how many people might give you a few hundred dollars for the work you have done.

When you have a lot of people signing up for your site and for your newsletter, you will begin to see that all of those small donations can add up to a super payday for you.

You can even leave the donation button up the whole year round so that anyone who wants to make a donation when they're able can help you out.

HOW TO SET THIS UP

You can begin this process by simply going to PayPal.com and finding out how to install a donation button on your website.

It's a simple process and will take only a few moments to do.

This will then be linked to your PayPal account for you to transfer any money you make to your personal bank account (or that of your parents, if you can't have one yet on your own).

You can also provide the email address where your PayPal account is located and ask people to send you donations that way.

All they will have to do is:

- Sign into their PayPal account.

- Go to "Send Money"

- Put in your email address.

- Type in the amount.

- Send the money.

They will get a receipt, if they need one, and you will be able to see the money in your account, almost immediately.

OTHER PAYMENT OPTIONS

You can also choose to take other payments, like checks and money orders. These can be a little more difficult to manage and they also tend to be more difficult to track.

If you want to take these payments, it's best to only take them from people you know, like friends and family members.

7 - HAVE OTHERS TELL YOUR STORIES

Just when you thought you could hang up your online adventurer cape and go home, there are just a few more things you can and should do in order to market yourself online.

But this time, others are going to do the work for you.

GET OTHERS TO HELP MARKET

It all begins with looking for people who seem to already want to help you. These might be friends, family members, or just people who are excited about your website.

Why not recruit as many people as possible so that you don't have to spend all your time marketing and others can benefit at the same time? Everyone can win when you just take some time to look at who's available first.

RECRUIT YOUR FRIENDS

Your friends want you to make money because then they can learn how to make money.

Tell them that you will give them something every time someone tells you that they heard about your company from that friend. The more your friends can bring customers to your site, the more they will benefit, and the more money you can make.

Recruit your friends to:

- Tell people about your website.

- Take about what you're selling.

- Show others what you have to sell.

- Talk to the TV stations and newspapers.

- Talk on forums about how great your business is.

Your friends can be a lot of help and since you're going to give them an incentive to help, they're going to be very helpful.

ASK AROUND

You can also ask others if they have heard of your business. Just the simple question can be asked if you're on the bus, on a train, in a mall, etc.

When the other person tells you no, then you can tell them about your business, hand them a business card, and answer their questions.

Or you can spend time just hanging out with other people your age and ask them if they would be interested in hanging flyers or handing out any freebies that you might have to hand out.

You'd be surprised at just how helpful people can be when you offer them something in return.

MAKE IT WORTH THEIR WHILE

What can you offer them in return for a friend or stranger's time spent marketing?

- Give them a free item.

- Promote their business on your website.

- Buy them dinner

- Give them a gift card.

- Give them a percentage off at your store.

There are a number of things you can give to people who are willing to market your business. The gift doesn't have to be expensive or huge, just something they will like having.

WHAT ARE AFFILIATES?

What you might not realize is that when you recruit others to sell for you what you are doing is recruiting affiliates.

These are people who are affiliated with your business and who are committed to seeing it succeed. They are going to be actively marketing for your company, encouraging others to buy items and to be a new customer.

The affiliate program idea is so powerful that there are actually whole websites and companies devoted to setting up affiliate relationships online.

Some of these include:

- www.OfferVault.com

- www.affiliateprograms.com

- www.affiliatewatcher.com

Or you can do the work on your own.

SETTING UP AFFILIATE RELATIONSHIPS

You can also create affiliate relationships on your own by talking with other website owners to see how you can help each other out.

All you need to do is:

- **Come up with a system for fairly compensating each other for the marketing the other does:**
  For example, you might say that each time an affiliate sells $50 of your stuff, that you give them $50 credit at your store.

- **Create a plan for marketing their items:**
  You need to make sure you are marketing their items and talking them up on your blogs and your website. The harder you push for others to buy their products, the more they will push and market for you.

- **Don't forget about your own marketing:**
  You still need to market for yourself as well as for others. Don't focus too much on marketing for someone else or your customers might get confused.

8 - YOU CAN TELL YOUR STORY

Your story as an online adventurer is going to become a legend when you begin to use the social media networks to talk about what you have to sell or to share with others.

From Facebook to Twitter, you can make sure that everyone in your friends list not only knows about your products and your services, but they also know what's new and what's exciting to you.

WHY SOCIAL MEDIA MARKETING MATTERS

Social media marketing is hot right now and EVERYONE is using it, from big companies to smaller companies, everyone who wants to succeed is using this sort of marketing to help themselves be seen, and so can you.

BENEFITS OF SOCIAL MEDIA

There are many different benefits to using social media:

- It's free.

- It's more casual.

- It's easy to configure to your needs.

- You're probably already using it.

- Your customers are already using it.

- You can reach customers around the world.

- You can set up an account in minutes.

Social media is not just for talking with friends or for finding out who likes who, you can use these programs to help your business begin to grow and to reach people you can't reach in any other way.

TIPS AND TRICKS TO MAKE THINGS WORK

You can use social media more effectively when you follow these tips and tricks:

- **Have more than one account:**
  You want to make sure you have a presence on all the social media networks.

- **Be active:**
  Make sure you stay engaged in the conversations when you are using social media. You need to use these accounts often.

- **Link your account:**
  Many times you can link your accounts so that you can have one post be seen on all of your accounts without having to type it in several times.

- **BUT, you should have unique posts:**
  Yes, it's easier to have the same post for all of your accounts, but people will realize this. Make sure you also include different posts to ensure that people aren't getting bored.

- **Use scheduling programs:**
  Programs like Twitter can schedule posts for you to be posted in the future. This way, you can always have something on Twitter and Facebook, even if you're not at your computer.

- **Use all of the business tools:**
  From lists to pages to groups and more, make sure you find all of the different options that businesses can use in order to spread the word.

- **Have separate accounts from your personal account:**
  At first you might want to use your personal Facebook account, for example, but once you get more comfortable, it's better to have a Facebook account for your friends and one for your business.

Social media is simple and easy to use. It doesn't take a rocket scientist to figure it out.

You can get started today with your personal accounts.

SOCIAL MEDIA OPTIONS

The list of social media options continues to grow as their popularity continues to grow.

FACEBOOK

 As the most popular social media network right now, Facebook is helping businesses and people connect.

You can use a number of different tools in the Facebook program:

- Pages

- Groups

- Status updates

- Link postings

- Picture postings

- Photo albums

- Twitter applications

You can set up your Facebook page to be ready to post any information you want to post about your business.

First, you need to create a business page by going to:

www.Facebook.com/pages/

Here, you will answer questions about who you are, what you offer, etc.

You will then create a page for your webpage, one that works a lot like your normal Facebook page.

You can post pictures of your products or you can just post status updates to entertain your customers and fans.

You can also use the site to talk with customers about problems or other concerns.

Use Facebook to:

- Like other businesses.

- Send messages to customers.

- Show customer new products before they go on your site to see whether they are going to be good sellers.

- Share your website link as often as possible.

- Write notes about your store.

- Share news links about related topics.

- Start conversations about issues related to your products.

- Share special discounts that only Facebook group members can use.

- Share pictures of yourself.

- Post instructions to items you sell.

You can use Facebook for more than just poking people.

You can share your business with a lot of people all at once, helping to establish you as a business people might want to shop at.

TWITTER

Twitter is another way you can interact with customers in a more personal way. In just 140 characters, you can talk about business, share links about your business, or pictures.

This is called micro-blogging and while it's little, the tweets can go a long way.

Here are some ways to make Twitter work for you:

- Post interesting tweets

- Post often.

- Include keywords in your quotes.

- Use hash tags (#) in your quotes with keywords: i.e. #frogs

- Connect to your Facebook account so you can post things all over.

- Interact with other Twitter accounts.

- Respond to DMs.

- Response to @ messages.

- Follow other businesses that do the same things you do.

- Use Twitter scheduler programs to schedule tweets for times when you're in bed or when you're not going to be at a computer.

Twitter allows you the chance to be engaged in short bursts of time, which might be just what your business needs order to stay on top of the online adventurer game.

No matter what social media options you use, people your age are going to be on these sites too, and since you already know what people your age want, why not go to where they are?

9 - ALL IN A DAY'S WORK

Being an online adventurer is hard work, harder than you might think, and while there are a lot of things you need to do to learn about online marketing, once things are set up you can basically walk away from your computer and still see money coming to your bank account.

Just because you're young doesn't mean you can't use all of the same tricks that adults do.

You have the knowledge now. So, why don't you go setup a website right now and put what you've learned to good use? You don't have to have a superhero costume or even super powers.

All you need is a sense of adventure and a book like this by your side.

10 – RESOURCE LIST

I've mentioned many resources through this book and thought I had better make a list of them here so they can be easier to find.

These resources aren't a complete list, they are just a few that I use constantly and confidently recommend.

Buying Your Domain

- www.GoDaddy.com

- www.NameCheap.com

- www.CrazyDomains.com.au if in Australia

Website Hosting

There is only one I have ever used for all the years I have been online and that is www.Hostgator.com

Website Building

If you would like my help building a website, visit mine and contact me www.AskIanRichardson.com

Online Printing Service

- www.VistaPrint.com:

Writers for articles

- www.Articlez.com

- www.Freelancer.com

- www.Elance.com

Email Subscriber Management

- www.Aweber.com

Where to post articles

- www.EzineArticles.com

- www.buzzle.com

- www.hubpages.com

- www.examiner.com

- www.akgmag.com

- www.eHow.com

Google Adwords

- http://adwords.google.com

Payment Processors

- PayPal.com

- ClickBank.com

- 2CheckOut.com

Affiliate Networks

- www.OfferVault.com

- www.affiliateprograms.com

- www.affiliatewatcher.com